I AM

A book of unintentional thoughts

By Alexander Jackman

Eloquent Books
New York, New York

Eloquent Books
An imprint of AEG Publishing Group
845 Third Avenue, 6th Floor - 6016
New York, NY 10022
www.eloquentbooks.com

ISBN: 978-1-60860-826-3

Printed in the United States of America

Book Design: Rolando F. Santos
Cover Design: Jacqueline Abromeit

I would like to dedicate my book to Troy.
I see the King in him and wish him Greatness. He has to take his lessons like the story of Troy. Learn to be strong both on the inside and out remembering that love not only says hello but goodbye as well.

A wise old woman once told me something:

A Prince is a King in waiting. You should find the difference between a Prince and a King and be that difference.

Roseann Ayton 20th March 2006

I love you both.
You have taught me so much.

As a token of my deep gratitude, I have used your names to serve as the identity of my work.

This work is a tribute to the love and effort put in to me by my grandmother Anora Alexander Jackman and Grandfather Leslie Julien Jackman RIP (17th December 1995)

I hope I have made you proud and your legacy can live on.

Alexander Jackman

Acknowledgements

TO MY NAN, you have been able to say goodbye to someone you love and move on with your life. I always felt that Granddad was the man of many inspiring words. Now I know that everything that he ever said to me came from you. He may have had the words but you lived it. Granddad, it is 13 years since you passed away and I would like to thank you for sharing some moments that I will never forget. I believe that to this day you continue to walk by my side like the footprints in the sand.

Mother, you have always been a mountain of strength in my eyes. If I have learnt anything in this life it is through observing you. At times, I have underestimated you and I am sorry; I could not ask a better person to be my mother. I love you with all my heart. This is for all the mothers who have been great examples to their children.

Father, I remember you always used to say that nothing in life is free. For years I questioned the truth in that statement. Only to return to the many times you made me smile without a fee.

Aunty Wendy, I have always looked up to you for inspiration, guidance and direction. When English was not my strongest subject, you endeavoured to help me through my difficulties as best you could. I could not have conceived this book without your encouragement and loving embrace.

A special thanks to my English teacher, Mr. Johnson, who said 'You will never be good at English.' I believed he was right, but I am still trying my best! My best is all I can give.

Nikky, my brother, I am proud of you and would like to thank you for some of the most important moments in my life. I love you.

Simone, Jozi and Marcus Daniel, you have become outstanding young parents. I admire your honesty and drive to always give your all. If I can be half as good as you three I will be proud.

Karl Daniel, you have shown me that hard work and dedication can take you anywhere you want to go. I wish you all the best in your new adventure. I remember the things we dreamt about as kids, you have made a dream a reality.

Rael, Davien, Amarae and Tayte you now have many examples in your life to follow. Choose your own path and become an example in your own right.

Dennis Mensa, are you a guardian angel? You gave up your position in a talent competition so I could speak... WOW! You are a perfect example of what is great about this world. Your sacrifice in 2003 has brought me to this moment, writing this book. Thank you.

I would like to thank Daniel Robinson for believing in what I was trying to do in 2003. Without that belief, I may not be in this position now.

Kerrin St Omer, the timing of you in my life was very relevant and pivotal in my development as a person. For that, I am indebted to you. You changed the course of my life.

Denika St Helen, thank you for your endless support and inspirational vocals. I will always look at those clouds in the sky.

Paula Robinson, you have been a Great Mentor to me. You helped me to get this book from manuscript to publishers. We all need a Paula Robinson in life at some point to pick us up, dust us off and carry us until we can walk again.

Monique Iqbal, you will always have a place in my heart. You arrived at the right time.

Louise Armoogum, you have played a role in the work that is very tangible, my book. It has developed immensely with your critical input. Thank you for showing your enthusiasm. Without you, I do not know where I would be.

Charlene Hope, my sister what can I say when your surname says it all! To my beautiful goddaughter Nyah, I hope I can make you proud.

Isaac Alabi, there is loyalty and there is LOYALTY and a GREAT friend! This is for Jordan.

Philip Anthony and Kingsley Iyoha, thank you for your ongoing support. You were there from the beginning.

Emma Samuel, you are a GREAT TEACHER with THE MOST BEAUTIFUL SMILE. The children at your school are truly fortunate to have you. If you do not leave your school to share your smile with the WORLD, I hope I can bring parts of the world to you to witness it! Your smile need not say anything.

I would like to thank Jacqueline Abromeit for capturing my imagination with a beautiful book cover. Kathryn Harrison, for putting up with my constant changes and the rest of the team at Penpress Publishers for every step they have helped me to take in this journey.

Finally, I shall never forget my First Love.

I write this in memory of Latisha Shakespeare and Charlene Ellis who died tragically in 2003.

Aunt Lilian Mcleod, who was born on the 7th March 1920 and died on the 6th August 2007.

'You may cry for a night but you will smile again tomorrow" anon.

These are my unintentional thoughts.

All my love Alexander Jackman

1979

Genius does not simply reside in the few,
but in all living beings

When I was born,
Like everybody else,
I wanted everything

Including a baby brother and sister

The tears and the sacrifice
Make me who I am today
The love of my mother is why

Mother
I thank you
For the person you have helped me to become

I remember sitting there watching
in awe of this grown man
How did his hands get so big?
How does he manage to stand up, walk?
Eat food
No help, no bib
He spoke in funny tones
I did not understand
Just smiled, that was all I could do!

Please promise you will stay
So that I can prove also
I can grow big and strong like you!

With everything in my now life
It all starts with poetry

My words will paint a thousand pictures

I have come here to announce my identity
The lion has returned to my heart
With the strength of Samson
Removing shackles from my name
A queen, palm rolls my life to my art

There is no room for Delilah
I expose my weaknesses to the blinding inner light
I see through the eyes of my children
In this age
Emerging from my shadows
With Locs for Life

[Inspired by my loctitians at Jay's Locs for life]

This is the first Garden of Genesis
Where Life, has been eclipsed by the mind
The Sun's rays descend to tell another story
Wet thoughts on the canvas of Time

Made clear by this window of truth
Preserved by a disciple of the arts
A pilgrimage of wonder protected from the rain
The gate opens and the journey starts...

[Inspired by Graham and his fine art gallery in Crouch End north London]

If I am honest, I do not really know why I am at this point. I am not entirely certain what I have to say. Who will listen? Who will actually care? I am here working with something I have little knowledge and experience about. Yet this something does not require knowledge or experience. I do not believe you can work towards happiness. It is here already in this present moment. Who is in this present moment you might ask? I AM.

This book of thoughts is my first; I guess I am a virgin to this audience. I lay myself out bare for you all to see as it was in the past and as it is now.

I now know what it feels like to hide behind the very words I lay before you. All I can say is that I thought I had answered many questions just to get here. Now that I am here, the same questions return asking for new answers. These questions have always been who am I? Who are we?

Growing up, it was not my desire to become a writer. How I got here was a result of writing every single day following a conscious decision in 2003, to see what I might be able to create. I write now with a peace of mind, it is my world away from home.

Since 2003, I have visualised being here, writing in this space sharing with others.. It is actually more difficult than I thought. I realise that every word is a product for scrutiny, whatever I create. I accept that. However, I have torn apart and put back together each word in this book in a vain attempt for perfection. Since I cannot measure perfection, I decided to let it be.

It was not a difficult decision to share some of my experiences. I am certain now, when I look back, that I have not been alone in many of them. I cannot profess to have had a difficult upbringing, like in any family there were some difficult moments that threatened to tear us apart; but I was loved by two amazing people who did their very best to ensure that my brother and I had as much love and fun despite our modest resources. This book may be the beginning of many, so please excuse me while I find my voice.

I want to share my journey with you, one that has had many twists and turns without any specific structure or clear direction. This is not a guide on how to be or find happiness. All footpaths lead to the same place. I only ask that you believe that it exists and to be aware of all the subtle moments that represent peace and love.

There are moments in our lives small and seemingly insignificant that shape, build or define our character. We recall them because it is what makes us the person reading this text now. However, there are moments that we simply brush under the carpet as if it never existed. I am prepared to let you into some of those unashamed moments that give you what you see today.

Before I began writing, some of my dreams had fallen away, so I guess it was a good thing I had a very welcome distraction. I was in love with a girl. It starts...

Real beauty is in the life we see as true

Memories of my first love

The Conception

Young immature and helpless

Already involved with somebody else
Who, I told the truth;
'I'm in love with another'
As I clear the dust off my shelf
To make way for a new beginning

Beautiful flawless skin
A smile so infectious you feel warm within
This is my brown suga woman
Loyal to the bone
Her soul prints play sweet melodies
Like the chords on her saxophone

Before

She intrigues me
I want her to be with me

What shall I say to her?

And after

Ahem... I like you
Do you like me?

If we had kids together, what would their names be?

How about Jet

JET?

WHAT? No WAY!
Are you mad?
Can you imagine what that would be like for her in registration at school?
I cannot do that to her!

So it is a she?
Yeah I want a girl first... they are more mature then boys and I am a boy! I mean MAN!

Whatever you say...

I like Kam'ron and Kamarni

Her university is so far away...
what am I supposed to do?
Write to her?

Why do you love me?
I know why I love you
I think about you, everyday
My heart thinks about you too

As every second
Of every minute
Of every hour passes
I have time to reminisce and dream of another life I wish to share
While I am away

The Friday night
CONCEPTION

We made love by candlelight
I remember it very clearly
That night I held her so tight
I felt her whole life fizzle through me
Like I had known her in a previous life
Our beings were one together
Could I have made love with her twice?
A rendezvous match made in heaven

Did you? Did I what? You know? NO!
OF COURSE NOT! WHO DO YOU THINK I AM? I WOULD
TELL YOU! I AM NOT THAT STUPID!
(What have I done?? Please, please do not be pregnant)

The morning after

FLUSH!!!
OH NO

WHAT?

I HAVE JUST BEEN SICK!

WHY?

OH

WHAT HAVE WE DONE?

Okay, do not panic. We will get the morning after pill. However, it is Saturday and on the weekend, the Health Clinics are closed. We have to wait until Monday and that will be too late! What are we going to do?

YOU TOLD ME NOT TO USE A CONDOM

WHY DID YOU LISTEN TO ME!

I DON'T KNOW

YOU'RE THE MAN! FOR CHRIST'S SAKES!
YOU SHOULD KNOW BETTER!

SO, this is SUPPOSED TO BE MY FAULT...

YEH... WELL IT'S DONE NOW

... Anyway you cannot get pregnant if we have unprotected sex only once... or when you are on the pill

MY MUM WILL KILL ME! Actually forget my mum! WHAT ABOUT MY DAD? THIS BETTER WORK! OTHERWISE YOU ARE DEAD MISTER!

YOU'RE ON YOUR OWN ON THIS ONE! I DON'T WANT TO BE A MISSING PERSON

TICK

TOCK

Baby I really think I'm pregnant
Don't lie? ... Is it mine?
Not funny
Get a test, I'm not paying for it!
Look BOY don't get me started right now
Maybe I should wait a few more days I feel like it is
coming
I am scared
We'll be fine... (I hope)
Do you think we should tell anyone?

On my mind

If she is pregnant, what am I going to do? How am I supposed to provide?
I need a miracle right now. I cannot tell anyone!
How much talking are we supposed to do? It is not making the problem go away!
My parents are going to be so PI$$ED!
I can hear them now!
Are you ever going to be responsible? How are we supposed to trust you with anything?

When I think about it, we never really spoke about sex!
It is a bit late now!

HOW AM I SUPPOSED TO TELL THEM? WHO CAN I TELL? WHY DO I FEEL SO ALONE? NO ONE CAN POSSIBLY UNDERSTAND. PLEASE, I PROMISE IF SHE IS NOT PREGNANT, I WON'T HAVE SEX AGAIN! HOW COULD I BE SO STUPID?

THE TEST is

BLUE LINE?

What does that mean?

Where is the instructions?

I threw it away!

Why? You are so stupid!

I think we are in the clear!

How can you be so sure?

I don't know

NO!
KEEP IT.
We CANt
we ArE nOT rEaDY
It would not be fair
wE hAvE nO cHoIcE
Now her young blood stains the walls of our hearts

Please don't tell your mum! I don't want her to think badly of me!

A Lost goodbye

I look at this woman lying next to me
I'd keep watch of her at night
To guard her silent thoughts
I could never explain the tears in her eyes
I cannot truly know what she is going through
I was not even there when she needed me
How could anyone make a decision like this and remain strong?
Like it never happened
I know she will never forget
She may never forgive herself
I know I will not forget
I do forgive her
It is my fault...
Deep down
There is no blame
I feel like I have failed her
She would not change me for another
Yet I still have the cheek to question despite everything!
I need to trust her more
Give her more credit
This is not about me
It was days ago we spoke of having kids together
We did not actually mean now
Her eyes are open
It is pitch black in this room
I cannot sleep

Why is it
When we are close to death
Our lives have so much worth
Why is it?
That we take for granted the women
who are blessed with giving birth?

Kamarni

I always wanted a girl first
This is our little secret
I admit we made a mistake
I am sorry
Things do not happen the way we plan
I cannot forget who you are
I have tried to say goodbye
I do not know how
Maybe I do not need to
I do not want to replace you

One day I will see you
The blood on your baby hands have stained the walls of my heart

Her tears are rolling down my cheeks

Will God punish us for this?
Because I feel like those who follow God
WILL!

AAA
RRR
GGG
HHH

WHY ARE WE SO ANGRY WITH EACH OTHER??

It feels like

Anything I say is Wrong
Anything I do is Wrong

Aren't my thoughts to have a voice

I am mute beyond reason
This isn't the right time to be heard

Maybe I should say something...

You don't know anything about me!

But then neither do I?
Why don't I?

This is all my fault!

YES!!

THIS IS ALL YOUR FAULT!

I DON'T KNOW WHAT IS WRONG

I DON'T KNOW ME ANYMORE

This is not fair!

Why am I
here?

What has gone wrong?!?
I cannot explain it!!
Maybe our time has come to go our separate ways!

It's over!

Babes I miss you. I'm sorry

It's over

Give me back my stuff

Babes I miss you let's get back together

It's over!

Stop saying it is over!

...

It's over

You are not listening!

I don't want you in my life!

Furthermore, don't talk to my family!

I'm sorry too, let's get back together

Whatisshethinkingwhatisshethinkingwhatisshethinkingwhatisshethinkingwhatisshethinkingwhatisshethinkingwhatisshethinkingwhatisshethinkingissheseeingsomeoneelseissheseeingsomeoneelsedoesshelovemedoesshelovemedoesshelovemedoesshelovemedoesshelovemeigetsomadwhenshedoesmakesusarguewearguebecauseofheritisnevermyfaultsheisalwayswrongsheissospitefulwhatisshethinkingwhatisshethinkingwhoisshewithwhoisshewithwhydoesntsheanswerthephonewhyisshenotpickingupherphonesheismakingmeangrysheisdoingittospitemeohlooknowshewantstocallmebackiamnotgoingtoanswerherphonecallandseehowshelikesititreallyisoverireallydon'tcareanymoreicannotbebotheredwithallthisrubbishidon'tlikethewayshetalkstomesoihavetoraisemyvoiceiamhurtingrightnowishouldhavepickedupthephonewhenihadthechancemaybeshewillcallagainphoneisringingitisnotherwhydoesshelikeputtingmethroughthismiseryithinkwecanworkitoutbutsheneedstolistentomeandstoptryingtothisissoannoyingmaybeiamthinkingtoomuchamithinkingtomuchihavearighttothinkwhatilikewhoisshewithgoodshehasansweredmyphonewhyisshelaughinglikewearenothavingissueswhoisshewithicanhearamansvoicethisistearingmeapartwhatamisupposedtodofineiwillhavefuntoosowhenshecallsmeicanlaughdownthephonelikeiamhavingfuntoohahahahahahahahahahahahaahahahowdoesthatfeelnowitdoesntfeelgooddoesitthatishowyoumademefeelicannottalknowiamhavingtoomuchfuntobetalkingtoyougoawayidontcarewhatyoudoohnowshecaressheiscryingshehadahardtimekeepingthatupimsadifeellikeishouldnothaveputherthroughthisiamsorryihavemissedyousomuchyoudonotunderstandicannottakeitwhenweareapartifeltlikeyoudidntcareaboutmethewayyouwerelaughingandjokingwithyourfriendsstoptellingmeitisoverallthetimeicannottakeyoudoingthatitisnotfairyoudonotknowhowitmakesmefeelwellstopputtingthephonedownonmewhenyoudonotlikewhatihavetosaythatissorudestopslammingthedoorstopthrowingmythingsoutassoonasyoudonotlikemeihateitwhenweareapartyoudrivemeuptthewallwhatdoyoumeanidriveyouupthewall?whatareyoutryingtosaydoidothatallthetimeyesyoudoohforgetyouthenifiamsuchamenacetoyourworldyouknowwhattodowithyourselffinethenidonotcareiffactwhydontyoujustleaveicannotstandthesightofyouyougetonmylastnervegoodbyeandgoodriddanceyoucanforgeteverythingisaidtoyouiwaslyingdonotspeaktomeeveragainyouaresoimmatureimimmaturethatisfreshcomingfromyoumorelikeyouareimmatureandchildishforthatmattergrowupnoyougrowupfinejustleavemealoneiambetteroffwithsomeoneelsewellyoudojustthatseeificarewhateveryouthinkyouownmewellicandowhatilikeandyoucannottellmewhattodoclicknosheneverputthephonedownonmeiwillringherbackandgiveherapieceofmymindoicannotbelieveitshediditagainiamgoingoutofmymindicannotlivewithoutherwhatisshethinkingwhoisshewith

SILENCE!
YOU
THINK
TOO
MUCH!

It's over!
STOP SAYING IT IS OVER! I HAVE HAD ENOUGH I CANNOT TAKE IT ANYMORE!

Look, it is obvious you two love each other you both are being petty!

I don't like it when we keep breaking up!

I'm sorry.

It's OVER for GOOD THIS TIME!

Babes I love you let's get back together
I have missed you so much
I just do not like the way we keep ending things as if it means nothing. I hate us arguing all the time!

What is the lesson I am supposed to learn here? I do not understand! Someone please help me!

I am certain I already know my lesson I am just not strong enough to do anything about it?   and I don't know why?

I think the only thing you can do right now is write.
Maybe that'll take your mind off things!

Okay, what do I write about? Think...

STILL
NOTHING

Breaking News
Two innocent lives were caught in a cross fire in the early hours of 2003's New Year's celebrations in Birmingham

Their names
Latisha Shakespeare and Charlene Ellis

The MEDIA say blame HIP HOP
The POLITICIANS say blame HIP HOP

HIP-HOP MUSIC is to BLAME
SO ARE VIDEO GAMES, BLAME BLACK ON BLACK
CRIME... the hoodies are criminals

It is not Hip-Hop, neither is it video games. Is there such thing as Black on Black crime? I wear a hoodie, I play video games and listen to Hip-Hop. I am not a criminal!

Why do we obsess with finding things, or people to point the finger?

WE, MEN AND WOMEN ARE ALL TO BLAME!
We have forgotten who we are!

We do not know our neighbours names!
We see each other as statistics!
We identify each other by colour and nationality!
If a child is not the same colour as us, it is not our child!
If we did not have a hand in conceiving a child, it is not our responsibility!
I guess we have every right to kill them or let them kill themselves!

The blood of each child is on our hands!

While we murderers run free!

WOW that is powerful you need to share it... How?
With who? With the WORLD!
HA HA Very funny!

And the winner is............

ISSUES!
With the
The murderers run free

?

What the hell?

Who am I?

Wow
I can't believe I won
Do you realise there were hundreds of people voting for you
to win
Okay, it wasn't quite the world
At least it is a start
You are a POET
They call you ISSUES
That is what you speak about
It is easy to remember
You need to give that name a meaning
Meaning?
Like what?
How about
Individual Self Searching Unconditional Enlightened Soul?
I like that, for now...

You must have done something right
Why didn't I write before, surely there is more to come
Am I even that good?
Maybe I was lucky
WAIT
How can you say that?
You spoke to people
And beat singers, rappers, comedians and dancers
How is that lucky?
I still need to know.
Maybe I have spent so much time in love with someone else
I forgot to be in love with myself
I need to see if I am good at this...
Maybe this is who I am
I need to know for certain
I need to be on my own
But I don't want to lose her
I could end up losing myself if I don't
I love this girl I know I do!
Do I love me?
Surely I don't have to let her go
No
Yes
No
Yes
No
Yes
No!

I need to find me

We grow up believing we can move mountains
Only a few do
Maybe if we did the moving
The mountains would have no choice

Broken fingers

My heart seeps through torn skin
On my hands
As I think about where I'm supposed to be
Nervousness snatched from the jaws
Of my mouth
Numbed by the pain that is holding me
Back
From realising my potential
Back
I do not know my own worth
Back
Others see it more than me
Back
To wanting everything at birth
These are hard times now
Like the words that diminish from my lips
I have this dream I do not want to let go
My belief rests in the sores of my fingertips

What is it about you
That makes me, me?
Is it me
Or is it you?
If only I knew, what I do know
The vision is clear
Through the reflection
ISSUES is standing right there.

[An Individual Self Searching Unconditional Enlightened Soul]

So
why
do I
feel

like I
have
to let
her

Go?

I have made the

biggest

mistake of my life

It is probably for the best

When I was young

He passed away, another father I knew
A lost promise
To share me God's words
What makes the day turn into unforgotten nights?
What makes the soil of this earth?
What makes people come together in tragedy
and separates them in search for power?
What makes our hearts say we love and we hate?
Those words missed his final hour.
I miss him.

[Inspired by Mr Leslie Jackman RIP]

In everything,
I tried to do
I tried to be
In every way,
I tried to live
My poetry
Got caught up in this black hole of
My mystery
I wonder why it has only now fixated me

IT'S OVER I AM SORRY

A broken heart is like the bones in your body. When broken, they only grow back stronger if you allow them to heal properly in solitude.

Where is he?
WHO IS HE WITH?

Written by my first love...

Why does my heart feel so heavy like I have never been loved? Known love? I know this is not true because you loved me once, you still do, but still I do not see it, appreciate and feel it.

Why does my heart feel so heavy? As though I have never been loved,

I look at the person I want to love me and get nothing back, I look in the mirror and see nothing there, no love, no me, no love for me by me.

Could this be my curse? If so, what to do? Maybe, maybe I should just love you. All I ask is a response to the feelings I feel, a sign, an omen, please tell me what is the deal.

I sit here confused, thoughts running wild, all I ask for is a hand, please be my guide, I must take a breath, clear my head and my mind. Start again, slowly now, what could be the cause?

In the mirror I stare, too much I compare, the beauty I see is not only within, but beheld onto me, flawless on my skin.

I am beautiful this I must see, a person of substance, talent and glee. Why am I so hard on the one that is me? This is not the way I was brought up to be. I am doing the best that is found within me, and someday, someone will appreciate me.

So again, I ask why my heart feels so heavy, as though I have never been loved.

Now I see the answer lies within and above.

Real treasure can be found in the depths of a woman's heart

Waking up with deep visions
Listening
Making decisions
Christening
Baptised in illusions
Glistening
The moment she left my life
So false was my happy gracefulness
My thoughts always displayed distastefulness
I looked at myself disgraceful
When
She hooked up with this other guy.

Is it not obvious I am unhappy?
But I am unwilling to do anything about it because I am happy this way

You passed my eyes like a stranger
Felt like I've seen you somewhere before
Took a look back, when we once were closer
We could have been so much more

The grass is only greener on the other side
If you fail to take care of the grass you are currently occupying!

Lost Imagine Chocolate Relax Angry Luck Simple Touch Dance Water

Her tears were lost
On her chocolate skin
Angry
She made some mistakes
Ran out of luck
Looking for answers
Desperate
She will do what it takes

She relaxed her mind
Imagined a journey
That was simple
It allowed her eyes to see
As she danced with her reflection on water
She remembered who she was
Eyes opened
Touched by new possibility.

[Inspired by words from Chanelle Banton-Smith]

I became the writer, the poet, the performer - ISSUES. If I only spend a tiny fraction of my life being this person, doing these things then it is not who I am. Instead, I call this my...

False Dawn

Looking into your eyes
I can see a horizon
Far reaching but not impossible
Beyond I see a naked field
Awaiting our bodies to clothe it
I see passion radiating that field
And your eyes lighting it

I saw her
I never knew her
Her face was glittery
I want to do her
She has not felt this
I want to melt this
Temptation is a forgiven hell kiss

Perfect Rhythm

My hands run all over
Her hourglass figure
Erroneous thoughts signal
A stream through my fingers
Tight pressed against her hips
A melody played in movement
Squeezed up against her body
Tension rain down we're grooving
Too caught up in the moment
To notice anyone around
Deeply thrust each other perversely
Body suited to the ground
Intense concentration
Wet thighs and hard lows
Out manoeuvring each other
Synchronised by hushed groans
Tempo slows right down
I feel some chemistry in her eyes
I want to touch her in secret places
Make her eagerness subside
Lay a hot tongue on her naval
Cooled down by fine wine
Tease and caress her landscape
A short breath as I cross her line
Release her inhibitions
Open her gates for her passion to flow
A huge interest obeys her wishes
Slowing it down like Bobby Valentino

A glint in her eyes
A short whisper in my ear
As her soft lips, tell her own story
Came with intentions to fulfil a desire
My coated fingers as she moaned do you want me
Heightened emotions a passionate glance
Broke through as I thrust with my fire
I want more as she riddles in private
Playing with the chords of the telephone wire

I awaken, something's wrong,
I have been restrained
Imprisoned by cream finished walls
I am contained
Purple silky lingerie
Caressing all my zones
A stereo quietly playing
Melodic tones
My eyes close again with a smile

Fly Vision Emotion Sex Bus Chinese Frame Past Glass

He felt her heart fly away from her lips
As she exhaled his soul from her frame
Gripped with emotion it made her skin shiver
Touched by the sex with no name
It began on a journey by bus to nowhere
Her face glowed when their eyes met through the glass
Like they had walked the Chinese wall
In another life they shared
Their bodies rested while this vision relived their past.

[Inspired by words given from, Marina Lolita Hart]

Tenderness has this place of rest
Its symmetrical touch is moist at best
Yet the sensation is poignant and addictive to taste
As I reminisce about the kiss
Having left you at the staircase

Her

I just want to squeeze her
Tease her
Manipulate and heat her...
See her
Be with her
Have arguments just to agree with her...
Creep with her
Sleep with her
Show her love every time I meet with her...
Live with her
Breathe with her
Settle down and have my kids with her...

Love and Hate relationships

Wife: I don't think you know how much I love you
Husband: I'm sorry but I've been having an affair
Wife: What? You ****ing bastard! I hate you!

Her type

She tingles with excitement
As her thoughts are expressed in her keys
Fingers nervous, anticipating
A voice spoken on the page of her screen
She rides through a burst of emotions
Hot flush shift in her seat
Broad smile that takes her
To the peak of her existence
Divinity is where she ought to be
Romance on the tip of her moist lips
That at first was to pass the time
Soft torso bearing down on her bosom
Disappears in a moment
She tries hard to find

With everything I have experienced I think I can write a book
I just do not have the time to do it

Until the next time

She tries to talk to me by blowing in my face, biting my hands and whistling in my ear. She never wants me to leave but I would ignore her as I normally do. Nobody has taught me to understand her, I feel like I am teaching myself. Maybe she feels I am just not listening hard enough or I am listening but not hearing her.

She is so temperamental; I really find it difficult to know where she is going. Do I even know where I am going? We have known each other for so many years. She has caused me to fall heavily, promised to change. Even had hopes of taking me away with her and somehow I know she is only fooling around or is she?

There are times when she has looked after me so well and I have not said thank you. She has blown debris into my eyes just to see me cry. Why, when she has witnessed all my real ones helping to dry them every time?

I can only remember the few times she has been angry but maybe she is angry at the world and not me. I do not know. She has not said yet, I don't think.

I do know it will be difficult to imagine her not being by my side when I go for my next walk...

Island Love Life Man Lost Egg Pink Beginning Candle

His thoughts swam away with the tides of the ocean
Lost
This was only the beginning
Relinquished of his power
His mind stranded on an island
His life denied by so many different women
The gentle breeze almost blew out his candle
Like an unfertilised egg discarded by its heart
He rose again comfortable
Like a man clothed in pink
Knowing
He and love were never apart

[Inspired by words from Bianca Simpson]

It dawned on me late in this production that the reader needs some direction since this work does not follow the conventional rules for writing a book. There is no beginning or end, contents page or chapters just words. I give you a collection of thoughts in no particular order in much the same way we experience our lives or listen to our thoughts.

No matter how much we plan things we can never truly account for the unexpected and if we could what would be the point. Why am I writing? Well if I told you, I always had a passion for writing that would be a lie. I was in love with a girl and our time separated by university meant the only way I could fill space was by writing. At least until I had the opportunity to meet new friends. It did not take me long to realise that I actually enjoyed doing it, it has become my passion. Writers are not born they are made, made by love.

What is the whole point of all this? Simple answer there is no true and simple point. How many ask what the point is in their lives and are able to come up with answers that are specific and true for themselves? Well it is the same here. There is no straight path to getting wherever we need to be neither is it one-way.

Progression for many of us is moving forward. What is moving forward? How do you define it? How do you measure it? If over a period of time you gain financial wealth (moved forward) then lose it all, are you still moving forward? How relevant is it really to our existence as human beings since we take none of that away with us when our time is up?

This age is moving forward, technology and maybe our way of thinking. Consider this... A child in a conversation with his teacher at London's Lancastarian Primary School asked, 'Why do we have so much war?' His Teacher replied, 'people fight over land'. The child thought for a moment scratching his head before asking 'Why do people have to fight, is there not enough land to share?'

What you have here is a prelude to my desire to write full time. I can truly appreciate the sacrifice writers make to forge an established career. So, if my writing has any substance then the point of this will take care of itself.

I hope there is something for you as there was for me.

We do everything with complication
When life has never been so simple

Unintentional thoughts

Out of the darkness

An Individual Self Searching Unconditional Enlightened Soul

7 July 2005 in London

Choked by the darkness
That invades lungs
Ears blocked
I hear pain in whispers
Movement captured by
Flickering lights
Damaged cables
Dismembered arms and fingers
Feeling claustrophobic in the crowd
Ask me how I couldn't tell you
Why my nakedness is clothed with
Trauma
That stains the pictures of closed eyelids
In queues of panic and body-less aura
Short recollections unwanted goodbyes
Blinding lights lead us out to safety
All being significant for many different reasons
Yet relief
As our worlds have changed me me me me
me me me me me me me me me me me me
me me.....

[In memory of those who lost their lives and those who have to live with this experience]

Uncomfortable silence

I have never liked uncomfortable silences
For the first time I have no words to express
I feel a deep void has separated the two of us
As he,
Comes to terms with her death
We have never really spoken about emotion
When was the last time
I saw a man cry
I know strength comes from loss
Of a significant other
In his eyes, it was not the right time to die
I sit here watching my phone with anxiety
Tears are the last thing I want to evoke
The subject of sorrow resonant
On my tongue
Yet the words are even more so remote
Why do I feel so uncomfortable?

I have no place there
Why am I here?
They have left me all alone
When I was born,
I had the potential to do anything
Now that potential has gone

No different

Can you spare me 50p, blud?
Another soul passes by
Resting on their laurels
No money for the guy
Employed in the same spot
I am always asking why
While I'm feeding his addictions
His choices feed his lies
Plastic bags fill his soles
To block out the rain
Currency fills his mind
To block out the pain
He probably questions life
With everything to gain
So I guess we are alike
Somehow one and the same

[Inspired by a man called Gary]

I want to be stinking rich!!
Great! Woo hoo! Yeah!
....
So why can't I be bothered?

Vulnerable

An echo of addiction phones through for help
But nobody really understands.
Lost in translation,
Euphoric heights
Juxtaposed
With hell's sinister plan
Feel hopelessly suicidal the louder they're unheard,
Deafening ears and numbing their own pain
Only answers can settle their grievance
With this world,
Until then the anger will remain

[Inspired by a young woman called Coleen.S and a young man Karl.T 26.10.2005]

Knowing the answer and being the answer are two different things.
But what is the question?

A cocktail of life brushes
The hair of my nostrils
Unpleasantly
Telling the story
Of where he's been
Subtle murmurs pungent
In deep Arabic tones
That unsettles children
In the front seat wondering
Who is he?

I cannot possibly imagine
What it is like to lose a brother or son
I do know when they are gone
It is hard to replace with another one...

The Beholder

Her language of pain
Is thrown with a fist
She feels different to everyone else
Blistered features despite relief from her nails
Confused does she hate herself?
Tormented by smiles
With cotton wool hands
Her face drops when charity donates the words
That falls at the balls of her feet
Feeling beautiful is never too late

I saw the smile on her face
And sadness in her eyes
She had a different story
For each tear she cried

[Inspired by a melody]

Eat

Gaunt like features
See through eyes
Heart worn
His legs are weary
Have no reason to see out this life
That is governed
When he is not thinking clearly
Emotional neglect
A lost place in himself
Relationships disappear
Like his fire
He has no bones
Constantly eating himself
Regurgitating half his being
He retires
Until the next day

Find the light that can shine in your darkness

Runs Dry

Salt-water streams down
The side of a mountain
For weeks
I do not know why she cries
For once, she feels like she cannot move
Her heart disappears with the night
Not even the sun, rain or snow
Have influence
They once had
Like in all the good times
I look at her magnificence
I wonder what is missing
The stream leaves the mountain dry

[Inspired by the first time I saw my Mother cry. She still is the mountain in my eyes.]

I wonder why those babies cry
Possibly they see through adult lies
I wonder how those babies know
And I don't?

It is amazing when the opportunity is there
We will embrace it
Yet when it is time to look for opportunity
We cannot face it

The inner voice

Labelled as outcasts
We do not understand
Limited by the conditions of man
Afraid that unseen has no name in this plan
Only God comprehends and the few believe
Discarded because those gifts are unbearable
Never given the voice they deserve
Who are we to destroy cries embedded in ones now
When all they want is the chance to be heard
Not necessarily understood

Born on a blue day
Yet absent of his emotions
His number six was that sad place
Cold and dark
A desire to feel
Everything that they feel
In the mind
But not in the heart
I see his world
Built by numbers
An infinite code
That I understand his life to be
I too, look for my name
In that library of gods
When it is there
I feel
It will complete me.

[Inspired by Daniel Tammet on Richard and Judy show 17.07.2006 he is an extraordinary man]

In life, there are many things we take with us when we die

Conscience Failure Man Teeth Dance Music Love Contradict Attached Harmony

A splash of water
Awakens his conscience
Past failures reflected by chance
'An old man resides'
A soul with no teeth
That once had the energy to dance
To her footsteps the music
A floor made for his queen
Where love for him
Would contradict the now
Attached to one's arm
She has left him behind
For harmony where life takes a bow

[Inspired by words from Louise Armoogum]

Real success is measured only by your efforts to see things through to the end

Red Swim Sky Blue
Night Stars Space Sea
House Mother

After I first laid my eyes on you
I had this funny dream
Stranded in the middle of the sea

Far away
I see a house
That is where I want to be

How can I get there?
I have no boat
I know I cannot swim

The blue sky smiled at me
The answer was obvious
The red sea would part for Him

So I waited until night
Looked up at the stars
Hoping a miracle would fall

Somewhere from space
She held my hand
Walking side by side, she was beautiful

On our journey
We did not share a word
It felt as if we met somewhere before

She is the guardian of my dreams
She cleared a path to find my light
Like my mother, I loved her so much more.

[Inspired by words from Christine Abu]

This was not your regular one night stand
It was not about sex
I had only met her moments ago
This was more than your coffee routine
This was about reminding a lost soul
The only touching that occurred would be
That I held her tight
Comforted her until she fell asleep
I only listened
And understood
I refused to frustrate her with my logic
Or emotional detachment
I may never see her again

In the morning
We just kissed goodbye

This is why you are love
You caught my eye
And my soul yearned to know who you are

She saw him and everything she imagined this moment to be it was, perfect in every way. Her lips parted in admiration, her eyes had finally witnessed. Her divine truth only she knew for herself. Those few seconds raised the great hope that enriched her soul. He is the one. She whispered but he could not hear her although if he wanted to he could read her lips. He intrigued her, she felt compelled to know who he was ultimately who she was. This showered her with confidence to do what she has never done before, speak first. It went against her every rule. She was not about to let this moment go.

She took her first step and realised there was no turning back. She trembled towards the answer to her many questions. Is this moment real, can I feel this way? I do not even know him.

Her words quickly became a language she could not understand. Her heart gathered pace. She fought hard to suppress her feelings of anxiety and love. It was as if she was hungry yet afraid to take the first bite of a good meal. It began to rain but she felt like she was already in doors wrapped up warm by his fireplace when she spoke her first word.

Hi...

This is why you are love
When your real voice talks to me
I cry
I know that it is God who speaks
That's why when you open those lips
I take in every word you say in hope
That you can move me like that again

Built up by the nights expectations
A rush of heat radiates her cage
She cannot wait to be blessed
By an aura of silk
That caresses the smile on her face.
Nerves crush her humble existence
Embarrassed that time does not seem to care
If only the night could be as perfect and beautiful
As the hours she spends on her hair.

[Inspired by Caprius Hair Salon, Kingsland High Road, Dalston]

Healing

This is one of those moments
Where time is frozen
The healing begins its race in the vein
A known intuition penetrates the skin
Interacting with the pulse of the brain
Condensation inside the window
Of the third eye
Induced sleep by hypnotic state of mind
Witnesses gather to see other gifts of love
Once ignored by the egos of the blind

Her lines detail the past steps of her life
Like she has lived it in so many different ways
Her surface is flawless although she has aged
She works throughout the year, for every day
Strong roots penetrate the soul of her entity
As she branches out to blue skies above
Her purpose to recycle everything that we created
in ignorance
When all she does is Love.

[Inspired by Anora Jackman]

Although love may run out of time
Time does not run out of love

Every morning she gets on the same bus
Her goal, to walk the stairs for herself
Her legs are too small
She cannot comprehend
How adults can do it, without help
Straight to the front and onto her tip toes
Her arms reach for the windows ledge
To pull herself up
In hope that she too
Can see the whole world and forget...
How beautiful it is?

[Inspired by the baby girl that gets on my bus each morning]

Biography Sex Intervention Music Flowers Confidence Standards

Stripped of everything that has made me
This is my biography
My life
Like the flowers that respond to the music of the world
With the confidence of sex in natural light
I wait now for the one intervention
True love has already been felt
I stand out in the rain
Arms outstretched in my nakedness
Raising standards with everybody else!

[Inspired by words from Miranda Gravesande]

I still do not know who I AM?

What is it about me?
That makes me, me?
Is it me?
Or is it you?
If only I knew, what I do know
The vision is clear
Through the reflection

I AM

I AM

I exist
So she exists

[Taken from a conversation with an Angel]

To be continued...

LaVergne, TN USA
28 September 2010
198784LV00002B/16/P

9 781608 608263